AMERICA AWAKE!

We've Had All We Can Take

**Theory and Illustrations
by Karen Kellock Ph.D.**

A new theory in psychology. According to Koestler, all landmark theories are presented in picture-strip format (right-left integration) to bring on the "aha" experience of the formula (the characteristic of all new paradigms).

FORMULA FOR THEORY:

**ALL SUCCESS ATTRACTION
ALL DISEASE OBSTRUCTION
ALL RECOVERY ELIMINATION**

**The three obstructions are:
people, habit and food.**

**Remove your obstruction and
you snap to your goals,
waiting in the wings.**

AMERICA, AWAKE!

Must see what people are really like behind the mask. Don't feel mean, it's an incredibly beneficial task. To get to success divide from old systems keeping you down—a necessity before receiving the crown. Learn to recognize fake-friendly: You're "family" until you don't buy it (won't deny it) then you're ostracized--*believe* it. If you fit you're not legit but if you don't it may mean you're God's kid. Emotional Illness: a trauma happens they can't deal with so they eat/drink in excess to cover the mess.

PREFACE TO *AMERICA AWAKE!*

The meritocracy is going away as "white supremacy" to be replaced by boring woke hierarchies.

With God each day can be a brand new beginning but only if you geographically relocate I think.

God gives us a whole new beginning, white as snow/no shadow but people hate that you know.

I wasn't victimized by them but my own weakness letting them in. The world's crazy, gotta block em.

MERITOCRACY VS. BORING WOKE HIERARCHY

Boring woke hierarchies based on skin color etc. vs. exciting meritocracies of the clever.

If they find out you're not woke enough they'll instantly reverse to the other side with you out.

Had I just said I was scared to death of them they woulda left but I was milquetoast about it/they won.

Because the dumbed are the majority they feel strength in numbers while the superior man is alone.

Life's a journey and it started way back then honey--you let em in/you're to blame for the treachery.

The matriarchs of your new family will either welcome you or see you as a threat--watch out.

Most marital unions are rife with toxic family members , narcissistic/envious/hateful relatives.

In laws: Alcohol/drug abuse, meddling, generational curses--all kinds of demons in haunted houses.

Envious/territorial sister in laws or those bent on destroying your sacred union, it's all one.

Biden: "More humane policy" means they won't enforce the law and that's broadcast across the world.

CRITICAL RACE THEORY

Too much education impedes natural instincts. In our era Critical Race Theory is such a case.

Critical Race Theory [hating anything white] is a cultivated taste and war against best.

Critical race theory is cultivated irrationality which moved science to the side. Bill Lockwood

Critical Race Theory is a bitter vindictive hatred of anything white, like success or math.

Conformity is the jailer of freedom and the enemy of growth. President John F. Kennedy

Meltdown: one traumatic event after another getting weaker each time sucking you under.

While fasting it's most productive to just look out the window. Nothing tracking the mind below.

It is most productive to look out the window and not a waste of time. It's a fertile anarchy inside.

Jezebel would get her flying monkeys against me so later they'd be cross but she'd remain nice.

Anyone she brought seemed to hate me while she was innocent. That's the flying monkey set up.

Here she was coming to my home and all the while inciting other people: God, come!

FLYING MONKEY INSECURITY

In getting her monkeys to do her dirty work she has no control and they are far more cruel.

I was imposed on by inferior people because I lacked boundaries or the ability to assert them.

The women were extremely using, always borrowing things or officiously usurping/gossiping.

Give em an inch and they'd take over. They would make rules and break them, very underhanded.

I should be leaving all this behind, the people world. But PTSD keeps me hooked, looking for pearls.

I lacked boundaries coming from a fused system. To gain this muscle God allowed all this to happen.

Gave em a hookup for their RV & they spent all their time hanging here cuz I lacked boundaries.

And thus ends 130 volumes on How People Make Us Insane. Very little of it is inner-driven.

Gave em a hookup for their RV and they brought all their friends too you see, not even thinking.

I couldn't leave my front door with out bumping into her brother, lover, neighbors, things.

Gave em a hookup for their RV and they knocked on door daily to charge cell tho' I didn't use em.

ASSERTION OF BOUNDARIES

I didn't have the nerve--MUSCLE--to say "No, go to town to charge your phone, I wanna be alone".

After going thru all that with people I'm leery as hell. Betrayals by evil kin teaches you well.

They coulda killed me, they woulda killed me had it not been for Thee. Even in sin You saved me.

People insane in mental asylums over betrayal from a kin. An early trauma they couldn't deal with.

The event was so horrible, preposterous and unacceptable she went into lifelong denial.

This toxic shame which is passed on cam take the form of self-disgust for normal human functions.

God bugged me with people--total harassment--until i built the strongest boundaries possible.

The favoritisms, the polite cruelties, the coy treacheries can mess with your psychology for life see.

Fear God not life or the future. Cuz if you fear Him He'll take care of everything and it's forever.

It didn't please them when I went to their potluck, it was another and then another forever.

They're so lacking in inner reality/true self-awareness they urgently need each other I guess.

With all this going on they have short attention spans and this alone causes mistakes & negligence.

EFFECTS OF ALCOHOL

Being chemically sensitive the effects of alcohol were catastrophic but also curiously addicting.

Alcohol is a conduit to the devil. One drop, you dip into the collective unconscious of utter evil.

AMERICA AWAKE!

One drop of alcohol and lose all control. Even thinking about starting is insane/I'm done with it all.

A. A. terrified me as much as alcoholic hangovers. Social hebephrenia, boring meetings, no sir.

Only love of solitude & God and sick of the problems from this spiritual drought made me good.

The joy of early rising while it's still dark and not being hungover but excited for the new day.

A little good herb is fine, that's a right brain thing. But nothing up your nose and no booze.

Take one drink and lose ALL control of where it goes. Wake up in jail with absolutely no recall.

NEVER LOSE FREEDOM AGAIN

To NOT live in this world of social drama and control is so wonderful--do everything to keep freedom.

Violently territorial sisters in-laws, scapegoat triads, interlocking jealousy patterns: come God.

There's always the human element in family. Every system has a set-up, can you adapt honey?

Fall in love, get married and walk into a buzzsaw of violently territorial sister-in-laws. Need God.

Live a happy life with family then join a sorority and walk into a buzzsaw of social devices. oh my.

Devices to one-Up: I talked to her rarely but every time she mentioned I had a birthday coming up.

Fall in love, get married and gotta deal with his kids who hate your guts: the evil stepmother rut.

AMERICA AWAKE!

These are all sick human systems baby and I'm retired from it all luckily and live behind a gate see.

There was a time way back when I had to live under the same roof with that and them me alas.

It's the contagion of madness: we're infected by their mental illness, a deep split like a crevice.

Just cuz someone's a professional does not make them **NOT** mentally ill. Remember that girl.

I have a right to my mental illness as you do yours. The point is repentance and it's been years.

I had to produce to buttress up my grandiose self-image. It's ok to be conceited esp. if it's a big hit.

I couldn't be happier if we're on the same wave length. I'm inspired thinking you're reading my stuff.

HEALTH UPDATES

We live on sugar not all that shit. All you need is a little fruit smoothie to sustain--amazing isn't it.

Major obstructions are removed thru the colon then secondary ones as the vessels clean out.

I'm not saying all those foods are bad but that I can't take em anymore due to heightened total load.

Fruit smoothies with dates, **BLEND**. This is delicious and cleansing w/calories cuz we need em.

THE END

Dry years: Looked like nothing was happening but inside there was a fertile anarchy. Arthur Koestler.

The Lord was my champion, my support, my guidance. He brought me to freedom from "friends".

Queenship is knowing they can kill you and would, not taking anything for granted understood?

I'll be gone soon enough, I don't need you to remind me old girl--then you'll be the one in a stir.

You laid a helluva seed now get away. Take a vacay, finally. Stop writing or do it intermittently.

AMERICA AWAKE!

America is awake now. They jumped the shark, it's iconic: make your move, quick.

I've ignored the news cuz it'll only get worse. For the first time in history people choose the hearse.

It looks like they're taking over but they're not--get that through your head: they're false, dead, rot.

If they think you're evil, not just wrong--there can be no dialogue, only violence. Greg Gutfeld

The social justice warriors and anti-Trumps won't accept facts about inevitable socialist collapse.

The rest of us are gonna have to pay for their failed vision.

What makes us want Trump: Frustrations like long, tedious lines and social justice whines.

Cruelest dictators in history smiled all the time--that's the worst abuse as he drives in the knife.

Please help us Lord we're going into war: suddenly surrounded by strangers and many love gore.

No enemy is undefeatable. But to win we must face the evil not minimize it to prevent upheaval.

He who is devastatingly on target will be hated.

AMERICA AWAKE!

So much wasted time worrying when soon we will be dead. Only one life to live, be optimistic/happy instead.

This life (ball of mud) is temporary, suddenly we're old. But with Jesus we're ageless: we've made gold.

Age (should be): not a decline but keep getting better til the minute you die.

People are always going places while the inner suffers. All your time should go inside, getting tougher.

Traumas are a neuropathway in the brain. With each recall, peptides release-- repeating it in the main.

"Old" is a good term--it means sagacity. But when we take on the bad image we become monstrosity.

PTSD: You don't see the trauma (hell you went through) till after. Review it, suffer the memories, then laughter.

You must have self-worth for all you've been through. You were ruined, put through the ringer and scalded too.

Adapting to their mis-perception of me I lost my mind: stopped doing Your work and stopped being kind.

You've developed your art, you've found your niche. Took a lifetime of overcoming the rich/the witch.

Stay high no matter what. Transcend trivia but focus when you must.

You're now the best but it took years to get that way. Remember that, you deserve fortune--it's all ok

Any woman can be pretty, any man handsome: if well-groomed and on the right diet (no way to lie about it).

Unmet love needs create a bottomless pit syndrome of eating, drinking and other useless "filling".

You don't have to keep eating. Enjoy thy food time of 4-6 hours then fast all day: you'll be saying "hurray".

The most important thing about food is satiety power not nutrients but it's the same I think.

Dis-fatten and body loses the foundation of disease! Suddenly, everything's flat as disease melts like that.

Wrong food destroys self-esteem cuz things aren't what they seem then you can't discern fiends.

Photo-phobia is BDD: body dysmorphic disorder. This produces social isolation, the more as we get older.

I felt crazy, sought counsel. Then God said: "forget all that, just fast" and soon I felt good and special.

If one is photophobic he's on the wrong diet. Now just face facts and choose beauty for you can't lie about it.

The only cure for cancer is: get skinny.

You've lost your appetite—go with it. It's God's signal to go deep inside and you'll be loving it.

AMERICA AWAKE!

It's been proven that music and pet therapy is the highest and so powerful, use with caution (see journals).

How germane: It's pure synchronicity how it fits in history.

What aging's all about: looking back and mining for wisdom. To do this you need mental freedom.

There comes a time when you outgrow limitations of your origins: It's a mental thing and the block is sin.

The as-yet unrecognized genius has much to deal with--like being misunderstood cuza what he saith.

It's the greatest story ever told becoming a genius from a toad as the unique process (creative act) unfolds.

Learn all the rules of your trade in order to break them. In all fields that's innovation not lawlessness friends.

Creative Act is a structure in nature with beginning and an end: completion occurs then a new cycle begins.

I'd turn it all off cuz the important you'll hear again and again. Constantly return to nothingness then win.

When in sin you're handed over to the enemy. If you don't want control, repent and you'll have victory.

The simple social superficials are hot, the complex inward but unofficials are not but God loves them lots.

Communism means violence and Sanders loved revving up the dance.

Your sister loved Sanders, your nephew hated Trump. Time to forget family cuz that really sux.

It's clearly illegal to assassinate a president even in a mock way, like the beheading or the recent play.

She's "sorry" but whining about being bullied. That's the evil generation and she's still sullied.

She being bullied by the president because he said "You should be ashamed of yourself".

ALL that matters to them is that Trump loses. It doesn't matter whether we, they or the country does too.

Biggest pickpocket arrests from one group, biggest rapefests in another. Face facts though you're censured.

Facts don't matter anymore.

They're all for diversity except diversity of thought.

Hollywood celebrities are so boring, never original thought just towing the current line and imploring.

Everything the left does becomes stagnant.

For decades they've waged war on common sense and that is the reason for mass mental illness.

AMERICA AWAKE!

Liberals: You can't have open door immigration and not bring in terrorism.

She's an unbelievable traitor who doesn't know what she's doing--she's just virtue signaling.

If Islam is so wonderful why do Muslims seek refuge in Christian countries? Katie Hopkins

Islam is a religion and belief system that mandates warfare against unbelievers. Robert Spencer.

"Every culture's equal and you can't criticize them though they're pedophiles"--we are led by fools!

Burn everything down since you can't compete with great civilizations from the Renaissance.

"If we got rid of discrimination, ethnic divisions will heal". Bull, it isn't about that as the true facts reveal.

Donald J. Trump knows the only way to deal with ISIS is to unlock our military and kick ass.

To fight Islamic extremism we need an extremist (support Trump or we're dead, honest).

They cover Russian interference not Manchester slaughter of innocence.

As prosperity comes flowing back, the enemy throws everything it's got at it: that's globalism, fact.

People think that white people are wealthy cuz everyone else is poor--a false assumption to explore.

AMERICA AWAKE!

Trendies go along with anything but aren't truly friendly--that's the social game of the empty.

People are sick of it, they've hit bottom and the demoralization has backfired.

As moral laws weaken evil imaginations create weird freaks but we want Old Americana back please!

How exciting--we've now called the bluff of terroristic bullies. Alex Jones

Operation Expose Terrorist Media: Do it now, America!

CNN is a terrorist organization: Terrorizing, bullying and this type of Trump-attack promotion.

Virtue signaling on trendy topics to get approval from leftists--grow up idiots!

He's totally fulfilled promises but they said he's the biggest failure ever even before he pulled the lever.

Age of Anti-Intellectualism: facts don't matter. Split from the party line and it's daggers, agree and you're flattered.

Hillary cultists cry at her loss but not about any of her victims: utterly false, blasphemy, didn't happen.

ME GENERATION The devil in arrogance

Not just reflecting a generation but becoming the worst: more energy to fight or urge to sin of course.

The devil in you is arrogance. Pray you're sorry for how you were with the devil in you then have no remembrance.

Democrats of old were of the left but not traitors or embracers of a foreign ideology of death.

Thank you for getting us out of a 100 trillion dollar carbon tax and a loss of freedom by the globalists.

Let's all get together and make a deal and we won't lose our jobs or close our factories. Donald Trump

A trillion a year he saved us. Imagine what a rip-off this Paris Accord was.

The world has woken up: no more unelected global corporate government.

We are going to really look at the science and not listen to the overpaid pressure crew giants.

They choose dead Brits over being called "racist" and making em go back to Muslim countries: gist.

Both Islam and feminism hate sexy women.

Feminism and Islam, 2 greatest threats to America: one threatens security the other happiness and stability.

Migrants all happy pie in the sky then after they come in they're angry, presumptuous, arrogant, testy.

You must surrender to Islam and have your rights taken away or death: Australia

Hindus have lost 140 million people fighting Islam: why Indians love Trump.

Economic migrants from countries not at war.

Elect to take the best. Knowing what that is is half the battle then just do it: move to your crest.

Keep it a secret about your diet. It's no one's business anyway, that way you don't have to lie about it.

Daily vs. Festival Foods. All cultures have a two-speed life and a third for healing—how shrewd.

What is the sign of disease? acidity: white pastiness and bloat. That's because "acid causes mucus" Arnold Ehret wrote.

Bad food makes one acerbic: bitter, mean, nervy, phobic. He needs to change diet, not get a cathartic.

Much insanity is from being on a phony diet. It's more about that than whether or not you fry it.

The two greatest emotions are jealousy and feelings of treachery. The cure is diet and solitude: stability.

Pure food, clear mind: unlock ties that bind. It happens naturally as you clean the cells--what a magic find.

Whoever has The body wins the food debate hands down--but he who talks about diet with a big gut = clown.

He went to a restaurant and was constipated for three days. You never know what's in it, ok?

Soy in everything is constipating.

Just say "God I want to lose weight" then follow His instructions while never taking the bait.

100 trillion dollar carbon tax: Paris was pure chicanery but we have a national savior from dummies.

Agreement: Spy on every action you make and selectively shut down key industries: freedom was at stake.

A tiny group of armed elites living behind gates vs. the rest of us crowded into city ghettos in dire straights.

They act like globalism is superior. But it's totalitarianism, torture, tyranny-- not a pretty picture.

Trump's taken their foot off our neck: what a hero! This is as big a victory as the end of World War II.

Trump is not a servant of poverty, failure or death nor a persecutor of children and that's his sin?

The population bomb will ruin our home, safe as a womb. Everything they touch is destroyed like a tomb.

They're taking the houses based on fake taxes and giving them to illegals. It's globalists--kingpins of evil.

They said they will use border crises to bring tyranny in. A great time of misfortune and doom, again.

They have their vision of how the world should be and are gonna force it whether we like it or not.

Whenever one has power over you, expect them to use it for arbitrary purposes. Russian saying

Paris agreement: less about the climate and more about other countries gaining financial advantage.

We can't build any new coal plants, but China can--according to this biased agreement against Americans.

China and India could double their coal production but we're supposed to get rid of ours--none.

I cannot support a deal which punishes the U.S. but no obligations on the world's leading polluters. Donald Trump

Trump's so much better than the plutocrats who want to dissolve our border for cheap labor.

America is being taken over by multi-nationalists. This is the new colonialism making life impossible.

Socialism is: Waiting 8 hours for anything you want and that's on a fast day. No liberties, but hey...

A free market (when you let up regulations) brings a boom: Elation and prosperity coming soon.

Hopefully this exposure of recent surging socialism will bring a swing to pro-Trump support vs. Islam.

Liberal Russophobes have no problem with nuclear North Korea's dangerous case of missile envy.

Elites set up communist states then propped up those countries giving them everything out the gate.

AMERICA AWAKE!

Life is strange, sad, unpredictable and mad but music always saves me, changing things instantly.

What could be more therapeutic than 10,000 of your favorite songs listened to with cat or dog?

Things take longer than you think they will and happen much faster than you think they could.

As long as you're not working, just looking out the window thinking, you're most productive and happy.

How pleasant it is to come away from useless details! Cosmic peace never fails.

Watch as nature changes all day. It's so fascinating to live this way, part of the flow one might say.

It is so incredible that God can repair reality--change the past, even though it has passed!

Thank you Father I know You are always looking down over all my affairs, the only One who cares.

I don't like it when people modify with me. Man up--keep your appointments, please.

No I don't wanna go anywhere, No I can't commit to being there, No, No, No: the most important word.

The wicked are clouds without rain. They always disappoint despite their glitter/self-advertising.

AMERICA AWAKE!

The poser sounds so good to lame brains and hearts of wood.

I went through all that flack just for the raw data to later mine for pearls of wisdom: sages do that.

You've gotta push it forward now. Stop thinking and let the past go--you've got kids or pets, you know?

It's not a mental illness but a neuropathway in the brain. It's the groove that's gotta go, in the main.

Refuse to give into the fires of desire and it "pierces" the mystic center, wakes the serpent/ lights fire.

As the serpent unwinds and goes out we lose compulsion and become part of the flow again.

You've proven yourself so now just be the magic elf and put the boring mundane world on the shelf.

Can't take it anymore, wake me when it's over but loved being together.

A point's reached where you can't track. Suddenly no books or movies--just your own map.

A writer never says he's gonna write soon, he just does it. Of all these false starts and fake fluff, dump it.

They're so outa grace they make wrong decisions: Holes in their bucket despite wealth/education.

Stop wasting precious time on time-fillers. Make hay while your sun shines, God said to be tillers.

AMERICA AWAKE!

The Paris Accord was a giant redistribution of U.S. wealth to other countries, and the liberals loved it.

We have abundant natural reserves to uplift millions of workers but they'd be locked, blocked, stopped.

American small businesses are booming so stop your whining you liberal know-nothings.

We're in this together--globalism's taken all our freedoms. Trump hates one-sided trade deals, amen.

The globalist-funded "elites" hate outsiders: They despise independents with common sense.

We had only worm status—no say, no way—in a global policy to destroy our sovereignty.

Competition breeds out bad: capitalism is self-correcting, communism is turgid/entrenching.

Capitalism rewards the bright and energetic, communism rewards the dull, lazy and pathetic.

The self-hating pathological white guilt has stripped our defenses against being milked.

It's the Islamization of America combined with the criminalization of patriots long since forsaken.

Welfare for migrants: not generosity but lack of commitment to Americans.

Say what you want, radical Islam runs islam today and is it's orthodoxy.

Under the Paris Accord we'd send billions to countries that had taken jobs away from us already.

The U.S. under the Trump administration will be the cleanest and most environmentally-friendly on earth.

Green Climate Fund: Nice name but it redistributes wealth out of the U.S. like 400 billion.

The whole idea behind the climate change nonsense was to take America down.

Soak the resources, pit us against each other, create huge complexes to track and carry out their plans.

If you want prosperity elect someone who doesn't hate America or have it out for the West.

Success through conquest always degenerates and implodes--we're seeing it, you know?

Under Trump the world will be rid for good of globalist deals destroying nationhood.

Trump'll get us outa the woods where the globalists took everything we owned just cuz they could.

They hate Trump cuz he's nationalist/Christian and they wanna takeover through globalism using Islam.

Refuse to be programmed by whatever the globalists cook up.

Getting the body you want is an achievement. So do it: not just for the weekend but forever, amen.

Now you can do this thing: be a lean, mean machine. Dissolve all superfluity, thin out, get sheen.

You'd be a fool not to be scared, we just found out no one cared. Now just fast on air to stay prepared.

Nutrient density equals satiety: what a nifty thing: Potent yet tiny meals are so incredibly elevating.

It is superior to live on the best and spend $25 a week. It is inferior to spend a fortune--how bleak!

Satiety is efficiency. Being sated I'm happy, content and focused on other things making my heart sing.

I fuel-up in the morning and then that's it. I don't see why you have to eat food all day to be legit.

It's an achievement getting the body you want. Only high metabolisms eat the croissant and still stay gaunt. If you want sugar eat fruit if you must.

Jesus is in on this thing with me but with Him it's a personalized diet: take the rudiments then twist it.

He is our healer, our health, the all-sufficient one. Don't depend on diets, they are deception.

I followed diets too and was miserable. Let God guide you each moment for your perfect health.

Economy not based on competition but shutting down competition and giving it to friends.

Withdrawal from the agreement is a re-assertion of America the mighty's sovereignty.

Why should the U.S. penalize it's economy, apologize and lead with it's chin while others do nothing?

The skeleton of world government was the carbon tax, selectively-enforced to screw us of course.

It's a takeover using socialism and Islam as their operating system and it means our ruin.

Secret societies/meetings are not-ok. These trade deals are destroying our freedoms--it's tyranny.

They're not trade deals but takeovers as the sell outs get big positions in the new global government.

The global bankers meet in secret to destroy our lives. They wanna control it all: husbands and wives.

Dismay of the globalists: "We cannot compete with the American experiment--it's gonna spread."

Make America--US--great again then our influence is the model for the whole world, enemies and friends.

For many, welfare is Robin Hood: taking back what was taken from them--just like Mexi-Californians.

You can no longer say one is smarter than the other. That's bad, racist, hateful, from the gutter.

Why did they want us to stay in the Paris Accord? Cuz there's more money if we stay in, of course!

Dictatorship by clerk: little nobodies who couldn't get elected themselves come around as enforcers.

If serious about "saving the earth" they'd renegotiate biased terms, but will not--must capitulate or rot.

You say all churches are good when they're not. Some are great but the rest are rot/part of the plot.

Be scared but grateful when you do something here that would get your hands cut off there.

Don't call em immigrants just antithetical cultures: clash and torture.

"Any world order that elevates one nation over another will inevitably fail". Barrack Obama--bull!

European anti-colonialism is based on guilt, Middle Eastern on rage.

An epic battle happening right now between the forces of corporate world government and nationalism.

PRAY that globalists, Marxist communists and Muslim Bros Islamists get out of our Whitehouse!

Collectivism doesn't work, it's a nightmare and puts evil people in charge.

What are the globalist tragedies? Because they are diplomatically-immune, tax-exempt unelected bodies.

AMERICA AWAKE!

In everything you say and do, draw lines. Don't push the envelope but pull way back: now it's fine.

It doesn't matter how many times you failed or for how long. Jesus paid your debt--to Him you belong.

Pray God turns talents into cash. You must think like that—increase your stash while blocking the trash.

Though Satan roars of sins I've done (and thousands more) by His finished work God knowest none (so it's Him I adore).

It's not about rhyming, it's so much deeper. It's understanding contradiction and seeing the reaper.

Get some class hicks. We're losing stature as we see everything the same--a mix: adults acting six.

A poet can't say "i'll work from ten to noon". For it comes when it comes and you gotta make room.

Must adapt to the creative spirit, not it adapt to you. It may go on for days/weeks so you gotta be fit/in tune.

Separate to get the higher rate. That's your lesson in life and fate: first you must deflate (eliminate).

You're just gonna wake up in fame just like you always knew. Get ready: fast/watch what you chew.

With completion of the creative act we return to stillness. You turn it on, turn it off like it never was.G

Giving up an allergic food is life-transforming. That's how badly it affects behavior, looks and performing.

Eating once daily, things work for the first time. It's even more impactful than what I eat: what a find.

When bad food pollutes, the body dilutes by retaining water (bloat). RX: fast on your green juice.

When not eating the right foods, of course they don't digest. This causes flatulence, the real pest.

Every vet knows how the animal looks reflects his health. Do you look good (true wealth)?

High elevation: fasting 19 hours daily. Keep eating = sleepy, dizzy, hazy.

Moving to a higher altitude forced me to upgrade diet just to adapt, be undizzy and alert: fact.

Eat your fill then stop-eating past noon. Now enjoy thy day immensely--watch as this catches on.

Keep telling yourself you're fasting--pat yourself on the back. You stopped eating, that's a fact.

Fasting, I can be anything I want. It raises the bar and opens vistas: a savant blocking taunts.

We shouldn't say what diet, but God did say fast to heal it.

Though we shouldn't tell em what to eat, realize food can be a major sin blocking God's treats.

These things may seem subtle to you but they are tenacious.

AMERICA AWAKE!

They have nothing to say, going along with the "mazeway". They'll agree to anything, come what may.

Megyn Kelly the paid globalist operative: we see who you are miss.

We could have the best plan in history and the democrats would veto it. Donald J. Trump

Fake news: it clips, and misrepresents

Why they hate Trump: Betas just love seeing the Alpha fall.

The old paths make supermen but conformist modernity really sux man.

It's interesting how people self-destruct. In denying their own instincts they conform, out of luck.

When things go dark, go inside. Ignore outer chaos, take it in stride. Tell it to God--only in Him confide.

They mimic each other, they chirp. They eat too much, they burp. And when you get ahead, they usurp.

Men, do you like modern women? The good ones are rare since they're encouraged to have venom.

They're brainless yet "hot": could care less about liberty—the most important thing for which we fought.

The nerd feels like an outsider so easily becomes liberal: to be included/not hated he gets louder.

They're empowered by academia and Hollywood to be the bullies (so they aren't bullied as the enemy).

AMERICA AWAKE!

Seeing an old loser friend may be an anchor to the past you don't wanna re-experience, man.

The babies we've raised: entitled to perks, can't take criticism, tyrannical and they hate hard

I'm into individuals (genius) which is true diversity, not identity politics and the inevitable adversity.

Now's the time to become very selective. Let most pass so just the best is your elective.

Simplicity is the ultimate sophistication. Leonardo Da Vinci

It's the God of Miracles: showing up at the last minute (as history shows).

Why are you so sad, why so tired? Cuz you let in the walking dead in--those stuck in the mire and soon to expire.

Never mess with fools--the shallow who act tough and cool but when it comes to you it's a gag rule.

Nerds feel unpopular like no one cares. So they join the liberal commoners who are boring (not rare).

It's the Wounded Gathering Thorns Syndrome. As life goes on templates create their own kingdom.

The polarization is increasing exponentially. This is scary and as old friends exit suddenly it's eerie.

Leave behind false ties--the world of dust. An email if you must then leave yourself open to true trust.

Frauds: their final facade's about to collapse—that is the way of God.

They're not your friends who control, censure or block your words. These are ideologues and a curse.

Their low quality of life is their reward. Their low quality of life is their reward.

Let liberal indignation be part of your marketing strategy: "don't go see that" is advertising for free.

And what did the testimony of my homey James Comey show me? Baloney. Greg Gutfeld

Get this through your commie traitor globalist heads: you asked for it now we're gonna kick your ass.

No original thought there--just repetition of silly slogans conjuring their growing fears (not seers).

When you think: "I've heard this all before" you must not respect and realize you're with a bore--now soar.

We've tolerated lawlessness for way too long. Cast it all out and be thorough--have a new song.

They've made us so afraid to speak, to be arrogantly rejected by these creeps: the trendy clique.

It's hard to forge ahead as conservatives, to be bright and audacious cuz arrogance is pugnacious.

If "white supremacist" doesn't work they call him a pedophile.

Now we'll see an uptick of violence. Time to use the maximum powers of the presidency to pounce.

For cutting off his head he called it disgusting and that she called "bullying".

It's all the weak betas that have dreams of war.

Leftists celebrate baseball shooting.

How many leftists are on welfare and into being victims?

It's a deep state coup d'etat and Trump has gotta clean out the CIA.

The general public is out of it's mind. Look what they put up with not breaking from evil and the unrefined.

What liberates women is not feminism but the great equalizer, guns. Think: that's the only way, hon.

They're paranoid, training to see us as the foe. It's no gameshow as things escalate, you know.

They say you can't judge unless a perfect ace. Not true: laws don't change and we have grace.

They told us black is white for so many years now, our joy died but through Trump we're back somehow.

It's no longer a civil society if by stating your views you're beaten up, fired, banished, eschewed.

They say we're doing the rejecting and banishing when all we want is to live freely and unashamedly.

Obama wasn't getting results opposite to what he intended, he intended the results he was getting.

Hate packaged as love, intolerance as tolerance, apartheid as multiculturalism, Sharia as political correctness.

Governments are famous for staging events or misrepresenting but now the globalists are panicking.

"Terrorism" is labeled "gun violence" as they target the patriots.

Called "tough love" it's just being mean. When cold harridans rule the scene we feel demeaned.

They are darkness calling itself light. They feel superior though they are dense, not bright.

The failure of the democratic party to accept an election means destruction.

To the progressive "ends justify means" but no one sees the blood carnage in between: cold and mean.

If you don't want to be a slave then come out of your cave of laying down to tyranny and you'll be the rave.

History's rewritten to make us look bad, but it's US exceptionalism that quickened and made us glad!

They're in groups--identity politics--while we're alone and that's like our president despite his throne.

The saints feel lonely and hated. They must be told it's a sign of superiority, that their destiny is fated.

You cannot sacrifice truth cuz some will suffer because of it.

Through diet you can compete at any age. Escape the fat cage in a miracle and be all the rage.

The answer to insoluble situations is to fast--escape the matrix. Enter new worlds--block tricks, it's fixed.

We're told to be fruitful. That's no accident for the harvest is obvious: it's so suitable and plentiful.

Jesus made everything even the fruit, which is endlessly beautiful to be youthful and fight the brutal.

Not optimal (N.O.) designates the foods to avoid. Anything other than Optimal = make it a void

What's less worse--sugar or aspartame? The latter I wouldn't touch cuz fat and cancer isn't the same.

The sick may justify bad foods which affect the mental. It's a process to awareness: non-compartmental.

Daily Fasting gave me a whole new reality: the problems dissolved and I mused: "this is true vitality".

Just skip dinner. Above all dieting techniques I've found this to be the winner for getting thinner.

Fasting, I've never been so pensive. This is what I've always wanted: it's spiritually and mentally intensive.

These humans look like caricatures cuz the globalists want us dumb and dumpy cartoon characters.

Every diet will work for some people. But not all and that's the point: for some the results are evil.

Insanity of liberalism—a utopian view facts be damned--creates mental illness and it was me too, man.

The left is vacuous, empty. Though it all seems so light, glowing and friendly when it's tyranny they get petty.

56 million babies aborted and they could care less (don't even seem to know) as evil is totally supported.

How to Win: Divide a people, create false flags making them irate, come in as the savior/decider of fate.

It went on for decades until I learned the differences between liberal and conservative, in reality.

At the heart of the democratic party is MAOISM: thugs, the elimination of our basic freedoms, Islam.

They read our restraint as weakness until the point where genius becomes ceaseless meanness.

It's sick how the church leaders are justifying debauchery. On Christian morality it is pure butchery.

People have so lost their way they're even afraid of guns. The very things ensuring liberty--the true fun.

Stink: Mental slavery is having to view the world through how a priesthood tells you how to think.

The dam is breaking cuz they're finally realizing we tell the truth and they do not. We're clear, they're rot.

Since they're so brazen about reporting rumors as fact, we get paranoid: overcautious sad sacks.

Dumb permisasive liberals don't realize they're worshipping Satan and going to hell for their shenanigans.

Griffin's press conference: the most insane thing I've ever seen, Alex.

She tells us her life story and we don't even know her. She's the center of the universe: controller.

It's getting pretty bad when it's easier to talk to a secular than a church member.

Liberals: wrong theory, misapplied constantly to everything then doggedly sticking to it despite any facts.

Is it possible we could come back from the brink? Yes, these turnarounds all happen quickly, I think.

Don't petty-fog with stupid trivia! Be a bottom line person (less is more) with high standards and criteria.

They do smear campaigns on those with brains. A stake in keeping dummies lame, they make fake claims.

The milquetoast always sides with the majority, and this false power shoots down all else as heresy.

Watch old movies: keep your mind in '47 not '87 so you can think clearly and (unlike them) reflect heaven.

Unravel from the mental illness of the last half century. Return to reason, tradition and our history.

The right: reason, logic, history and facts. The left: feelings, emotions, victimhood and grievance.

AMERICA AWAKE!

Actors use their bully pulpit to spout off ignorance cuz they didn't have time to learn by chance?

They came at you with hate. It's nothing you did, you just thought independently and they got irate.

One gets clouded by the ardent voice of majority opinion which gets angry at those outside it's dominion.

The bully culture is everywhere now. Men in groups, women who snoop--find true friends (no sacred cows).

The social world is forced gaiety and jocularity. Wouldn't your rather be real through talents and being a rarity?

Though worshipped as booby princess she's really boss hog. When it comes to friends I'd rather have a dog.

American's aren't mean--sin makes us mean so anywhere there's tolerance there's also meanness, see?

Don't bother arguing with the left. For when it comes to goals and theories all is justified, even theft.

We're tired of violence in the name of partisan ideology. Liberals see it as all-okay in interviews today.

Granted extra legitimacy due to their color or gender to put down the other
Irony: If you're diverse you're allowed to be racist against whites

Dems think by polarizing us they'll win elections but we're sick of this ridiculous and obvious deception.

Arrogant rulers fall and arrogance always precedes ruin. Stay humble, be sweet: you're a shoe in.

It's sickening how stupid they are. They don't know who George Washington is or what started the Civil War.

Give up on them: they will never see. It's a mental illness of zombies but you want to be free.

Men of this world = poor little moths in the night. Psalms 17:14

Colleges losing money by catering to the loony

A growing tolerance for violence on the left: Instead of it being "deadly and illegal" it's just "inappropriate".

Violence: the problem is not Christians or Trump but the progressive left and it's penchant for force.

Both ISIS and liberals wanna force people into agreement. The similarities are astounding and unAmerican.

We patriots take crap due to Christian restraint, but at a point we're roaring lions: here come the saints.

Who rules determines if and when they come and get you.

Humans have been bifurcated into two sexes for 300,000 years and now in just six months it's a curse.

You've a right to choose what your sex is and deny biology: wow, this is a first in all of human history.

DIVERSITY IS CRUELTY

Mass immigration is underhandedly clever: the left found a way to attain power and hold it forever.   The narrative: Whites are oppressors and nonwhites are victims for sure.   Every single racial difference is due to racism not IQ or environment.   They make us hate ourselves, attack family, ruin culture, centralize government.   The churches push melting pot integration thinking it will end racism but it's pure falsehood ma'am.

CHAPTERS

DIVERSITY is _NOT_ OUR STRENGTH

GLOBALISTS ARE ANTI-HUMAN
WHITES WITH OUT-GROUP FAVORING?
THE WORLD IS REALIGNING: IT'S ABOUT TIME
THE RE-ASSERTION OF TRADITION
EVERYONE IS _NOT_ THE SAME
STRIPPED OF RELIGION, FAMILY AND GENDER
THEY'RE COMING TO TAKE ADVANTAGE
AS INFLUENCE DWINDLES SEEN AS "DESPICABLE"
HOW GROSS: FRANCE AND GERMANY THE BOSS
INVASION BACKLASH SURE TO HARDEN
ARREST MERKEL AND MACRON!
RACE REALISM BRANDED AS RACIST
NOT LEFT VS. RIGHT BUT LEFT VS. WEST!
WHITE MINORITIES: GENOCIDE NOT DIVERSITY
PEOPLE ARE TRIBAL VS. GLOBALIST BULL
GROUPS: MORE DIFFERENCES THAN SIMILARITIES
ECONOMICS DOESN'T MAKE EM BAD
LESSONS OF WHITE SOUTH AFRICA
SEGREGATION KEEPS DYING SPECIES ALIVE
SUICIDAL BIBLE INTERPRETATION: LET EM ALL IN
MORE IMMIGRANTS MORE DEMOCRAT VOTES
WORST PUNISHMENT: INTEGRATION
EVIL EFFECTS OF DIVERSITY
THREE NEUROSES OF THE LEFT
SKILLS-BASED HIRING IS RACIST?
U.N. PLAN: FIND A HOLE, INVADE AMERICA WHOLE
UN PLAN: A DISARMED DUMBED-DOWN POPULACE
HIJRAH MEANS DEMOGRAPHIC INVASION
THE SMART SEE THROUGH LIBERAL NARRATIVE
WEAPONIZED THIRD WORLD POPULATIONS
OPEN BORDERS IS TREASON
TRASH BIN: AFTER WE INVITED EM IN

DIVERSITY IS CRUELTY

Not Our Strength—Our Last Breath

Mass immigration is underhandedly clever: the left found a way to attain power and hold it forever.

Multiculturalism means we all die together. Katie Hopkins

The major narrative: Whites are always the oppressors and nonwhites are always victims for sure.

Liberalism: absolutely every racial difference is due to racism not inborn so continue to let em in.

GLOBALISTS ARE ANTI-HUMAN

Globalists are anti-human: make us hate ourselves, attack family, ruin culture, centralize government.

The Lord has fixed all the borders of the earth (divisions of land, sea and nations). Psalm 74: 17

We haven't lost our homeland--we're still here--but we may as well have, living in dread and fear.

Any mention of "race" and it's like a hot stove--they want everyone the same, kept below.

The churches are pushing melting pot integration thinking it will end racism and it's falsehood ma'am.

The churches want us all brown when God made us all different--this is falsehood again.

Globalist Gameplan: establish new societies that lack identity--culture, race, gender, you and me.

How would you like millions of strangers coming over your border? It's what's happening all over.

DIVERSITY IS CRUELTY

Shoved aside in own family cuz you're white while they put up a stranger who married in tight.

Age of Decadence: Defensiveness, pessimism, materialism, frivolity, no God, welfare, foreigners.

Great numbers of foreigners arrive at the end of empire weakening as old grievances are aired.

Border control still: the Obama hold-overs are incompetent, corrupt, and anti-law enforcement.

Africa: where obdurate tribalism trumps political persuasion and envy carries the day.

It's not that i don't wanna be with you, I just wanna be alone. KK motto

WHITES WITH OUT-GROUP FAVORING?

The northern Europeans have strong out-group favoring which becomes toxic/self-annihilating.

Reason for deficit debt today: providing first world services to third world pops who can't pay.

Having a strong in-group identity they're happy to use violence at the slightest resistance.

Be the immune response to the multicultural cancer destroying/eating away our countries.

Secularization is globalism but nationalist is Christian.

The west is the best and the reason everyone wants to come here is because of that. Gavin McInnes

France was always socialist and way left, look at the result: a migrant flood but still they're stuck.

My new picturestrip is OPEN BORDER: not that we want it but we have it and it's wreaking havoc.

DIVERSITY IS CRUELTY

It seems like a quiet neighborhood but in an instant things could change and they're all deranged.

The minute your walls are down inflows evil all around even though they seemed so quiet ya' know.

A known Marxist, completely false pope.

Pope: Open your borders, world government is good, need a world gov church, the family is bad.

Highest murder rate/stabbings and muggings: London is incredibly dangerous and frightening.

Come on in--as long as you don't stay, come el norte.

Trump ratings up not just about money but confronting global tyranny and the invasion by our enemy.

THE WORLD IS REALIGNING: IT'S ABOUT TIME

World is speedily realigning to Christian nationalist lines after globalist secularism and all it's crimes.

Export secular modernity in the form of globalized human/reproductive rights creating blight.

Things taken as a hallmark of decline and decadence are now seen as rights reflecting human progress.

Globalism driven by devices such as "disembedding" cultures or "detraditionalization" like vultures.

Traditional moral values are replaced by "life style values" where anything else goes too.

According to the left, Americans should be sickened and ashamed of the world's greatest nation.

All their sitcoms are of urban America, they care nothing for us country folk fearing things like Sharia.

DIVERSITY IS CRUELTY

We have two distinct cultures here: the urbanized liberal globalist vs the traditionalist heartland.

Globalist trendies care nothing for the rural, the permanent, the traditional with Christian roots.

Disembedding: The globalist device replacing traditions and cultures with secular lifestyles.

Trans-local consumer based lifestyle values replaced the traditional events we went to.

In the face of threat to a sense of place/identity/security people tend to re-assert religious markers.

THE RE-ASSERTION OF TRADITION

The re-assertion of tradition is a mechanism of resistance against secular globalization/what fun.

They can't protect global business while also protecting local customs, religions and traditions.

The liberal globalist pope disappoints at every turn.

Prison: being locked in with em. That's how many learned about borders and the necessity of fencin'.

Putin keeps the western church out: not just seen as secular but pagan, and I see his point here.

Russia sees us as reviving abortion (child sacrifice), and pagan marriages through gay rights.

Russia sees us as reviving witchcraft--think Harry Potter and also England, an invasion catastrophe.

The irony is: the vacuum feminism created has made women the victims of aggressive males.

DIVERSITY IS CRUELTY

A culture of weak men doesn't result in strong women, but unprotected women. Steven Turley

The battered wife of a feeble continent.

If we're gonna be a minority in our own country, what was it all for?

Ageism/Brexit: Forward-looking youth felt betrayed and victimized by elderly wanting to leave.

White flight = downward spiral of ghettoization.

EVERYONE IS *NOT* THE SAME

If "everyone's the same" disparate outcomes "must" be due to immorality like racism or slavery.

Koran encourages taking enemy women as sex slaves and also children so of course men love it.

Only 7% of Germans Nazis but look at the bedlam/lives lost. Same with Islam, it only takes less.

White ruling class with global homilists pushing a one world brown dystopia controlled by them.

The displacement of white Christians is a state-sanctioned dispossession.

Who's to blame is always "cuibono": who stands to gain.

Much of the stuff happening to white people has been buried.

Evil Globalists: Put all the disparate groups together then take control and end all their independence.

Globalist eradication of differences: so they can no longer discern nor express their own interests.

They have no homeland but feel they own the world.

DIVERSITY IS CRUELTY

Taking down our cultures then flooding Europe with millions a year with radically different values.

Across the world populism and nationalism is blooming. We can win despite millions flooding in/fuming.

Humanity is coming out of its slumber/trance.

We're to be a homogeneous world of mind-controlled atheists.

STRIPPED OF RELIGION, FAMILY AND GENDER

They seek to strip people of their religions, families and even sexual identities to make em zombies.

Those who do not block their borders will be lost. Viktor Orban

Millions are flooding in and millions more about to launch, this is historical and mass murderous.

Globalists flooding Europe with millions a year then weaponizing them against the freer.

Here's where we take a stand or we lose everything.

UK/Europe crisis: This is historic and mass murderous, millions of jihadis are flooding Europe.

Christians are gentle so who gets appeased? It's the old saying a squeaky wheel gets the grease.

Trump can't get into London but if you're a jihadist they pave the streets with gold as apologists.

A "nice" Christian man turning to Hinduism? Happens rarely but when it does, total destruction.

It's the fallen new age churches that want everyone the same color so "racism" will be no more.

DIVERSITY IS CRUELTY

Actually God made us all unique, also the nations. He didn't want a bunch of blobs/freaks on rations.

Do other religions give true peace, when terror looms large from error?

Churches wanting us all brown are workers for the New World Order as God made us unique/clever.

By saying "words are violence" they can throw you in jail for assault through your verbiage.

"Give me your tired..." is just a 100 year old poem by a socialist so please just shut up.

THEY'RE COMING TO TAKE ADVANTAGE

They're coming to take advantage of us because we are people who create wealth/they can't resist.

They're fleeing the hellish societies they created for themselves cuz they simply don't have it.

Wherever you see white people they're creating wealth and migrants want that for themselves.

They can't do it--create wealth--so they come here to get ours while putting us in a hell.

Diversity is not our strength, they're at each other's throats. It's just a utopian vision of Babylon.

Not wanting your people replaced is normal, natural and healthy.

We don't want riffraff hanging around here.

Whites have built the most successful, easy and pleasant societies in the history of the world.

It is not racism to say low IQ races are violent and rapacious, it's just a fact but you can't face this.

DIVERSITY IS CRUELTY

Democrats are now the party of foreign voters, many illegal. Tucker Carlson

Venezuelans dying of starvation as the communists pass a law saying you can't call it starvation.

Without parent approval kids now change their race not just their gender: mentally ill pretenders.

Carbon taxes are a cash grab, the latest liberal scam and fad.

Liberals hate western civilization and Christianity, it's key component/basis for our great nation.

There are some rich whites but most are poor as blacks so don't listen to the liberal flack.

In sum, they want to maintain their crazy third world ways but with a great first world income.

AS INFLUENCE DWINDLES SEEN AS "DESPICABLE"

As our influence dwindles in our own country we'll become a despised remnant seen as cruelty.

When liberals wakeup they flee the shit holes they create then escape to and ruin our red states.

Comanches tortured everyone they met so stop telling me about the sweet loving Indians, get it?

The only safe defection from North Korea is Christian missionaries cuz they're the good guys.

Proof we're at the end: Invasion by people not our friends to whom our own government lends.

They killed 80 million of their own people and you liberals align with the Chinese? Evil, evil.

Go ahead and serve your evil globalist masters, you'll be the first to go when they take over.

DIVERSITY IS CRUELTY

Diversity is nothing but the lowest common denominator making us hate them, him and her.

No worry, judge lets you off for rape cuz you didn't learn to respect women in your Muslim faith.

6 Nobel prize winners unanimous the diversity experiment has failed so let's go no further into hell.

600,000 migrants in Italy a social time bomb and finally they see it and jumped on the bandwagon.

HOW GROSS: FRANCE AND GERMANY THE BOSS

It's obvious France and Germany are the boss.

The EU wants obedient satellites but Italians say "enough is enough".

A Europe shaped like Merkel/Macron has no future.

To get your life back be a euro-skeptic.

Anyone who denies the current Islamization of Europe is an accomplice. Fratelli d'Italia

Saudi Arabia is funding it all: mosques, cultural centers and universities in the west, Europe, Italy.

Italy: What a shame to have fought wars for centuries against Islam only to lose it due to inaction.

The E.U. can go f**k itself. Matteo Salvini

Forcing unwilling populations to accept those now living amongst them.

Any new gov has severe repercussions throughout Europe--like deporting a million just like that.

A disunified angry increasingly intolerant populace coming to the end of their rope as an experiment.

DIVERSITY IS CRUELTY

Merkel madness will take a generation to clean up while she walks away and shrugs.

Expect the Swedenization of Ireland. It's time to object to globalization tactics, Irishmen.

Italy represents a massive shift to euroskepticism and the evil EU's end.

Brexit marked a massive change in politics cuz it's all about immigration, forever changed.

Youth voting for the EU--pee yuu

Brexit was the first domino and it's a tidal wave now.

Massive change, soft left political forces destroyed.

I think you've missed the point, but I thank you. Farage, Nigel

Don't take em in but divert money to camps near conflict zones so they return to family/country.

They come to west to breed us out while living on benefits and spreading Jihad--do you see that?

INVASION BACKLASH SURE TO HARDEN

It may be this invasion will harden the west/bring us back to the best and destroy liberalism no less.

She's devil incarnate, the most evil person who's ever lived in Germany destroying her own country.

Migrant crisis or Islamic insurgency nuisance?

When high IQ countries invade the west they get rich and don't blow things up.

Breakthrough: Relieved Europeans now want rapid action and know that a new Europe is possible.

DIVERSITY IS CRUELTY

Sanctuary state governors or city mayors are criminals and should be locked up now.

Sanctuary states protect criminals not citizens and thus they are gangster organizations.

Putting the interests of immigrants over citizens--that's how whacked out the left has become.

Truth is no defense in Canada because it may spark outrage against the invaders and more trauma.

They didn't start that way, dumb. It's from intermarriage with first cousins marking the whole region.

Every time a first cousin marriage the IQ down 15 points so the multitudes are really outa joint.

If Merkel isn't stopped Germany will not be German within a generation.

ARREST MERKEL AND MACRON!

Arrest her: Merkel is responsible for destabilizating the whole continent for generations to come.

The West doesn't have to be Merkeled if it doesn't want to be--we can stop this crisis now, see?

Diversity is a curse on any society. It erodes trust and makes building social capital impossible.

Guilt implanted: Even white men willingly wanna give up land to minorities who hate em.

Globalism destroyed identity/made us feel empty. Now we're refilling with symbols from our history.

Much new age drug and alcohol abuse was an attempt to fill the void left by globalism, annoyed.

DIVERSITY IS CRUELTY

Anywhere there is multiculturalism there is great sadness by whites on how dogs are treated.

The United Nations wants to reduce our population AS they flood us with other nations/religions.

Whites' anti-ingroup preference reflects in voting non-white to show you're not a racist blight.

Ireland is now the "emerald isle of Somalia"

Gender: It's NOT a spectrum but a bimodal distribution including effeminate men/mannish women.

RACE REALISM BRANDED AS RACIST

If you say it's inborn (IQ, intelligence) that automatically makes you a racist in their eyes I guess.

Communism: Rapists/murderers were put in charge since politics made them that way by and large.

Isn't it interesting how it's only white countries getting mass immigration from the third world?

Whites can't escape and white flight's declared as racism.

"Racism" is an anti-white hate slur.

"Diversity" just means less/no white people.

Immigration without assimilation is invasion.

In a low IQ society aggression is a strength and empathy a weakness so being peaceful fails.

With a cultural IQ of 80 and raised brutally will they ever be child-friendly? Not predictably.

Just be accepting of their harsh/crude ways. You don't wanna be unaccepting do you? Not ok

DIVERSITY IS CRUELTY

We are weak but reasonable and logical. They are strong and violent and die hard radicals.

The threshold of what is acceptable has been lowered and it's a scare as we've become cowards.

The Epitome of Bull: Diversity is a strength but if you dare disagree with me I will destroy you.

Harboring criminals is the left's screwy view of citizenship and if you don't agree you're a bigot.

How we're different: West is influenced by the Reformation, Renaissance and the Enlightenment.

NOT LEFT VS. RIGHT BUT LEFT VS. WEST!

It's not left vs. right but left vs. west.

The biggest thing in our history is mass immigration into the west from third world countries.

Tens of millions are ready to embark in our direction.

Using mass migration to abolish the nation-state for a super-state is not new but makes us blue.

A nation is not just birth and origin but a tribe and groups of people vs. mass dejection/confusion.

Get off my case you stupid snitch--instead of "witch" it's now "racist" and you're put on a list.

Mass third world immigration increases dependence on the state while not voting to diminish it.

Dumb populations vote bigger government and higher taxes, the opposite to views of patriots.

A nation is a people of order: there's a way we do things and it works (makes us happier)

DIVERSITY IS CRUELTY

A population voluntarily replacing itself is unprecedented in human history and insane, clearly.

Could you see Japan choosing to replace itself with another group? Of course not, they're not fools.

Fact: Willingly gave up your culture when ancestors paid with their blood to give it to you intact.

Just an idea: the left hates nations or anything but oneism--One Worldism--tho' it's a scam.

We have a rich history/culture and to give your children Mogadishu is the most evil thing to do.

WHITE MINORITIES: GENOCIDE NOT DIVERSITY

When white countries are filled with non-whites it's genocide not diversity

Left demonizes nationalism because it blocks their agenda and that's the bottom line in America.

To describe the Germans as white people with a common ancestry is a hate crime now--WOW.

Blatantly telling Swedes that it's not their country anymore and to make room for New Swedes.

No place to go if opening our homes to the world and it becomes unlivable, I know cuz I was a fool.

It's young males all over the world invading, raping and destroying.

Think of it: the gangs, the invaders, all the trouble is from young males.

If not cool with this total and rapid transformation you're a racist cuz diversity is our strength.

Whites celebrate their own displacement and everyone but their own people and it's unbelievable.

DIVERSITY IS CRUELTY

You can't change demographics of a nation without a cultural, economic and political transformation.

Israel to remain Jewish = cultural pride. White Christians want the same = horrible and denied.

They are seeing that socialism never works/goes against nature just as nationalism takes over.

People are tribal in nature--caring more for their own nation than a foreign nation, for sure.

PEOPLE ARE TRIBAL VS. GLOBALIST BULL

People are tribal--that's a fact--and some BS fantasy or utopian ideology won't change that.

Just a matter of time until EU collapses but the question is: how much damage in the meantime?

East Europe just got their country back from failed socialism they're not about to hand it to Islam.

Feminized girlie men and masculine women linked with evil satanic globalism for this invasion.

Karma for baffoons: Keep your eyes on Europe, things are gonna be very interesting soon.

Tradition is not the worship of ashes but the preservation of fire. Gustav Mahler

The fed up Germans call Merkel "Mother Terrorisa" or "people's traitor" shouting "lock her up".

Cold to begs and tears, Germany will take in more than a million new refugees next year.

Merkel keeps testing the limits of Germany's political consensus.

Our freedom they see as blasphemy, our logic is their hatred, our free speech they detest, furious.

DIVERSITY IS CRUELTY

Blasphemy laws only pertain to offending Islam, never Christian.

Price for multiculturalism: offending and being offended but blasphemy laws are only for them.

Blasphemy Laws are not to protect religion, but only Islam.

Blasphemy laws are Sharia creep.

Food line: Young male migrant pushes aside an elderly lady so German state calls her a "Nazi".

The liberals would call us bringing in white African farmers facing genocide "racist", you can bet on it.

When the liberals rule: recycled water from sewers ok'd for California taps-- wow how cool.

GROUPS: MORE DIFFERENCES THAN SIMILARITIES

The murder of whites in South Africa is twelve thousand percent higher than blacks in America.

The major race science claim: there is more difference between groups than within them.

It's the biggest genocide in human history, the final solution to the white Christian European problem.

You can only get into the UK if an extremist, non-extremists are 86ed. Muslims vote left in the west.

Go Trump, our most wonderful president, without whom the witch Hillary woulda let them all in.

Climate change is nothing but a man-made lie. It's just globalism arresting those who defy.

Stone age or primitive people in an unspoiled landscape isn't automatically pure, pristine they ain't.

DIVERSITY IS CRUELTY

In primitive societies the more they killed the more wives and children they had: the status of cads.

In current academia, conformity to orthodoxy takes precedence over scientific methods.

Pseudo science of "radical racial egalitarianism" is false but you're good if you adhere and evil if not.

Tho' totally false, lives are destroyed if they don't agree to perfect egalitarianism, truth betrayed.

Races' different diseases: whites have terminal cuckishness or pathological altruism for sleazes.

Atheists are radical anti-science fundamentalists and zealots.

Atheists have betrayed science, undone religion and opened up the west to this terrible mess.

Societies that treat women the best are dying off, those who treat them the worst are flourishing.

ECONOMICS DOESN'T MAKE EM BAD

It's economics that makes them bad so if we give em a house, car and cash they'll be nice instead. Not

Violence is from lack of resources? Most terrorists are middle class so how does this argument exist?

If the benefits dry up the migrants go back.

If you can't see a barbarian when it's blatantly right in front of you that means you're one too.

Women don't have children so they wanna mother the migrants. Stefan Molyneux

The better the climate the worst the government, it's a tradeoff.

DIVERSITY IS CRUELTY

If the Black Lives Matter ever got the power here, that is the government of South Africa.

We don't hear about white African slaughter so we see into the future like white minorities oughta.

They don't want us to see what happens with whites a minority in an aggressive, tribalized world.

We all know where it goes with anti-white hatred instilled: in a tribalized society they'll all be killed.

Appeasement is the hope the crocodile will eat you last but it's coming and it's hungry. Stefan Molyneux

African chances of stopping the anti-white snowball exploding diminishes daily and it's frightening.

LESSONS OF WHITE SOUTH AFRICA

If we don't learn the lessons from white South Africa it'll come here and we'll be the minority, betcha.

Is it true that white liberal feminists are maternal to dogs and migrants but hate their husbands?

When that demographic change occurs everything will be gone for us while they flood/surge.

The Omnibus Spending Bill builds walls for Lebanon, Egypt and Jordan but nothing for us, man.

Diversity plus proximity equals war.

Blacks and Hispanics have been begging for the wall cuz it undercuts their wages and no one cares.

Europe's current leaders and the pope don't react to this invasion as they did in the middle ages.

DIVERSITY IS CRUELTY

The term "progressive" sounds so sophisticated--that's why they like it--but it's just pinheaded.

The desire of whites surviving as a distinct people is being swallowed up by fear of being seen as evil.

What a predicament for whites and y'all: Having to make a moral case for your own survival.

Whites sympathize with cultures who's existence is threatened but not their own--what an enigma.

Whites very sad when the last speaker of obscure language dies but not about their own kind.

Every nonwhite country has the right to preserve its culture, but not white America that's for sure.

SEGREGATION KEEPS DYING SPECIES ALIVE

Segregation not integration is how they keep obscure dying species alive, but not for us whites.

Why are whites the only ones explaining why they have a right to survive? Diversity is white genocide

Of two races creating delightful charming places to live (Asian or American) why do *we* have to give?

Japan is for Japanese only, though many from the third world would like to come in and enjoy it.

Migrants don't see generosity when they see Europeans (do they ever say thank you?) just weakness.

No backbone to maintain what's theirs, nor the morality to keep birthright safely for their heirs.

We could be disarmed and destroyed due to our virtues, foolishly lavishing on alien users.

DIVERSITY IS CRUELTY

They have no desire to be like us but easily take everything we have and we just adjust, even gush.

Others have a right to have what we have and we do not have a right to keep it, what a gimmick.

Suicidal double standard where all groups can press for their bids but whites aren't permitted to.

Since they cannot explain racial differences they always say the disparity is from white wickedness.

It's the same double standard in Sweden: whites always to blame and the others all the rave.

The most curious phenomena is the number of whites who have swallowed this self-loathing.

Every nation considers itself superior to it's neighbors and every nation is right. French Proverb

SUICIDAL BIBLE INTERPRETATION: LET EM ALL IN

Good Christian nations let em all in. Suicidal interpretation of the bible.

Fooled to hell thinking it's a wonderful blessing to be displaced by people unlike ourselves.

Why he won: He promised to send home every illegal immigrant, build a wall, possible Muslim ban.

A race realist and white advocate not "white nationalist" but we deserve our own place as majority.

Merkel, Hitler--whats the difference except the former is subtler but it's still invasion/murder.

Low IQ is violence, high IQ is refinement.

The people who tell us how wonderful diversity is can escape it--aren't we sick of these hypocrites?

DIVERSITY IS CRUELTY

It's a derangement exclusive to only one group: Whites giving away what is theirs, the whole scoop.

When you get disparate groups into society it's no longer about ideas but theft and defense.

It's important that the left wants to import low IQ voters--wonder why they need the losers.

Hispanic immigration is the death of the republican party, small government and free market.

The rules are changing with immigration cuz they want big government and so what if we don't?

MORE IMMIGRANTS MORE DEMOCRAT VOTES

The more immigrants the more Obama-votes.

If you want small government focus on immigration as the more come in the more socialist/corrupt.

The problem isn't so much Hillary corruption it's that the democrats don't care/no compunction.

Democrats can say "diversity is our strength" because for them it's true--it's their voting base.

The facts are clear: the higher your ethnic diversity the higher your violent crime, vs. peaceful whites.

To get votes the left is willing to have people raped, assaulted, murdered, kidnapped, forsaken.

Left are power junkies living in gated communities unconcerned with devastation from policies.

They don't care who suffers with them getting more political power, the object of their addiction.

DIVERSITY IS CRUELTY

As government gets bigger as desired by invaders it continues to increase till you're 3rd world/deceased.

All over America, neighborhoods changed forever with no public debate.

For the people who live there, it's traumatic.

Diversity for thee, but not for me.

Anarcho-Tyranny: Refuse to control criminals (anarchy) so come down on the innocent (tyranny).

They just don't live like us and they say the same too, so what?

So many slaughtered disproving myth that: we're all the same.

WORST PUNISHMENT: INTEGRATION

The worst punishment: to be thrown in with all of em.

In the UK the Muslim rapists are always labeled "local residents", "Asians" or "Oxford men."

America: Do not fall as we have fallen, do not become the UK, fight for your freedoms every day. Katie Hopkins

Whites ostracized as others have ethnic identity/strong in-group preference but we aren't allowed to.

Elites don't suffer from mass migration/multiculturalism--they reap the rewards, we pay the price.

Young male migrants pushing ahead of an elderly lady and the Germans react by calling her a "Nazi".

They say since we benefit the most from it, we are unaware of it--white privilege = their narrative.

EVIL EFFECTS OF DIVERSITY

DIVERSITY IS CRUELTY

Elites don't suffer from mass migration/multiculturalism--they reap the rewards, we pay the price.

Whites ostracized as others have ethnic identity/strong in-group preference but we aren't allowed to.

Young male migrants pushing ahead of an elderly lady and the Germans react by calling her a "Nazi".

The left calls anyone for immigration restrictions as a "right wing hick" or a "backwoods nativist".

As mass immigration increases diversity it reduces social cohesion and civic trust: stop it or bust.

California's skid row is now a vast sea of broken people, rats and human waste. Katie Hopkins

They say since we benefit the most from it, we are unaware of it--white privilege, their narrative.

THREE NEUROSES OF THE LEFT

Three neuroses of the left: cognitive dissonance, narcissistic rage and psychological projection.

"Foreigners shall not in any way partake in the political matters of the country". Mexican constitution

Appeasement: The more we're threatened by em the more we pander to em.

We're supposed to let the whole world in then fight over scraps of our economy in a trash bin.

America is a battlefield and the battle is thru demographic change and population replacement.

"Foreigners shall not in any way partake in the political matters of the country". Mexican constitution

DIVERSITY IS CRUELTY

California's skid row is now a vast sea of broken people, rats and human waste. Katie Hopkins

Appeasement: The more we're threatened by em the more we pander to em.

Obnoxious liberal overreach on guns gives us a shot in November--I told you Trump was clever.

Anti-Trump prosperity and freedom haters would actually join forces with pure evil to dump Trump.

Our great president has a fifty percent approval and with his reaction to the caravan it's quickly rising.

That's our man, we must rely on him--don't let em in cuz the caravan would just be the beginning!

Invading army is approaching--did they hear about the massive spending bill? This is pivotal.

SKILLS-BASED HIRING IS RACIST?

Skills-based hiring is now racist.

Most of the people who voted for Trump aren't at war, they're at work. Michael Savage

They aren't churches they're dens of devils. Alex Jones

All left is radical by nature, wanting to destroy the social order.

Racism of the worst kind is saying you can only be racist if white.

Trump: Act now congress, our country is being stolen.

America is the problem, not the virtuous ones breaking in. We impede their progress so shut up/obey.

We're to blame for everything so let the virtuous ones in and they'll redeem us.

The new immigration is an army of people who don't bother with paperwork.

DIVERSITY IS CRUELTY

Hand the left a victory and they just move on to the next thing.

Tearing down statues is so sad as I'm living in a hyper-present tense with no connection to my past.

Trump has full authority to repel attack on the border. Ann Coulter

"We're rich, they're poor and oppressed--let them in!"

Trump has full authority to repel attack on the border. Ann Coulter

The caravan invasion is a test and an opportunity to see if Trump will react with {promised} integrity.

That crazy 2018 generation said there were infinite sexes and you could be any race you wanted.

U.N. PLAN: FIND A HOLE, INVADE AMERICA WHOLE

U.N. plan: Once they bust open a hole they'd invade, flood and take over the country as a whole.

DACA = democrat voters, power, lotsa money.

Oversaturated in leftist BS that everyone can come here, the caravan event cues wall (get-er-done)!

The reason women are lousy voters is the appeal to emotion and everyone knows that's a bad decision.

Women are lousy voters because they go for abortions, wear pussy hats and want open borders.

It's a matter of statistics what women vote for so don't take offense but it's something to abhor.

"Helping to save the world/charitable" when actually they're ruining the country/it's irrevocable.

Democrats have ruined every city they rule.

DIVERSITY IS CRUELTY

It's all about appearances with the left: to look like they're helping rather than actually helping.

Looking past their facade you can see democrats have no substance.

Trump using cashcow NAFTA to punish Mexico for being so incompetent and criminally dangerous!

SJW's don't care about genocide in S. Africa cuz they're white.

When liberals say they're pro-immigration they mean non-white, non-Christian immigration.

The globalist liberals want immigrants from Muslim or socialist Latin American countries.

UN PLAN: A DISARMED DUMBED-DOWN POPULACE

What they want is a disarmed, dehumanized and infantilized populace who is easily controlled.

The liberals want full global/media domination--they're globalists--and could care less about US.

Caravan pushed Trump for a stern and speedy response--Dems always do themselves in like this!

The caravan did us a favor: raising the issue to be seen as extreme and outrageous, it's a changer.

It's time for Daca to end/the wall to rise up, along with the American people who are sick of this evil.

Socialism is really creepy as people start eyeing your things. It makes one feel guilty/lives changed.

ISIS and Al Qaeda come into the US through Honduras along with Syrians so it's not just Mexicans.

The president is a dictator when it comes to the border and non-citizens.

DIVERSITY IS CRUELTY

It's a classic globalist attack to break up our sovereignty--we're five years behind Europe today

Trump has massive power at the border since it's the executive branch's main purview.

This demographic stealth invasion is much more permanent and dangerous than a Normandy-style one.

Roman Empire was taken down by refugees.

HIJRAH MEANS DEMOGRAPHIC INVASION

Hijrah means demographic invasion.

Canada is sinking cuz Trudeau was raised by a crazy feminist mom and distant dad: single mom kid.

Those who want diversity don't live in diverse neighborhoods, but are gated and protected.

See it as a pie: With each newcomer you are being displaced, your influence that much less.

We're being erased by being displaced but you can't see this not having empathy for your race.

928 machete attacks in London in just two months but mayor says it has nothing to do with migrants.

Macron plans to enrich French society by importing 200 million Africans--it boggles the mind.

The Swedish feminist praises Islamic polygamy and ignores dark sides for the utopian reality.

Macron plans to enrich French society by importing 200 million Africans--feel grateful, Americans!

In the world of multiculturalism and diversity, someone else's gain is always your loss, truly.

DIVERSITY IS CRUELTY

Theresa Mae: open borders advocate, phony feminist, virtue signaler, traitor to race/culture.

Why gun control? Because armed people won't get into boxcars voluntarily. History Lesson

Relax, you're really good in fact the best so just wait and fast.

Anti-Anglo is always dressed up as "anti-racism".

If you import the Third World you ARE making it more poor, dirty and divided but saying that gets you fired.

Is there nothing we won't put up with, with the bullying left and their cultural take-over? I wonder

THE SMART SEE THROUGH LIBERAL NARRATIVE

Don't tell me, I know the liberal narrative: You bought it whole but the smart didn't buy it at all.

God said "I don't wantcha working during days--just the mornings then no more focus (go to right brain), ok?

There's a CLICK as you switch from left-brain to right-brain or back again. It's ACTIVE vs. RECEPTIVE.

It's a DELIGHT to go from extreme focus (work) to relaxed/diffuse focus (relaxation and perks).

Takes me a while to relax after all that but music helps to make the switch to ECSTASY, bliss, excitement.

That's what you wanna believe but it's not science at all. Between races and genders there's total differential.

You have to memorize this new jargon to know what the human race is all about according to these louts.

DIVERSITY IS CRUELTY

Most older people are so lonely they don't care about privacy but boy that's not me, I want more each day.

Telling people about the historic world-altering achievements of white men can get you sent to prison.

Pride for your white race is now stigmatized by liberals, the media and establishment as a whole.

The narrative: white Europeans are the bad guys and everyone else must unite to cut em down to size.

Saying "merry Christmas" is so insensitive and divisive--said by mean generation throwbacks.

Suddenly I have high hip bumps called femme/sexy but where did they come from and what are they for?

I make em mad to make em think. It's in brutal reversals from their ordinary mundane world, rinky-dink.

Every other race without exception is allowed to be proud but not us, that's proof of our horribleness.

First let's state the obvious: our country is in crisis.

"Reform" to the EU means more centralization of powers, not less. So when you hear that word, resist.

Big mega corporations are allied with China and the communists, radical Islam and God-hating leftists.

It was hard to admit global government was tied to radical Islam or that they were targeting our families.

WEAPONIZED THIRD WORLD POPULATIONS

DIVERSITY IS CRUELTY

Weaponized Third World Populations: Because we forced these terms, the fight is on and not just Macron.

Humanity is awakening and the process is accelerating! All over the world yellow vests are protesting.

It's NOT the French government but an occupation by a group of globalist dirtbags led by a pretty boy.

If a leader brings in third world pops pooping everywhere then he's no better than a traitor/collaborator.

You have battered our people, squeezed them. They have a right to revolt/we'll arrest for treason. French Generals

UN Migration Pact: Even if a country doesn't want em in, they will force them in, white dissidents arrested.

TREASON: Open borders, announce to come here everything's free then your own people raped/killed/forgotten.

The UN Migration Pact is not legally binding but greases the skids for unlimited mass third world immigration.

Sweden has the highest crime rate in the world (whereas just ten years ago, the lowest) due to globalist traitors.

Once you believe a lie you cannot believe the truth. Only angry people believe lies/entire cultures too.

Gaslighting: "Just cuz you perceive it doesn't make it true"--questioning our senses about this big mess.

Everywhere a socialist gets in they become communist and it's always a nightmare scenario, honest.

Globalists concocted this whole operation of mass immigration pursuing a classless system.

OPEN BORDERS IS TREASON

DIVERSITY IS CRUELTY

Communism creates mass starvation.

It is your job to invade El Norte and take up residence in the United States. Mexico President Obrador

The Plan: People fleeing failing communism then destroy their new countries they reside in.

Flee collapsing communism in more than half of the nations then destroy whoever takes em in.

Like dominoes falling: they're fleeing collapsing nations only to destabilize new ones (like Chile).

You establish crisis centers where they're at not add military age men when only 10% get jobs.

Dominoes: Collapse Latin America into Mexico/Us, collapse Africa and Middle East into Europe.

Making their move to world government by collapsing third world pops into giant migrant waves.

Radical Islam allied with Soros-funded left and international combine.

Millennials overwhelmingly prefer socialism cuz they don't know what it is: disaster/utopian vision.

Do what the people want/voted you in for and you'll SURGE in the polls--obvious but not to fools.

We have to stop seeing ourselves as the underdog cuz we're not--we have the *peoples* on our side.

You feel vulnerable and powerless with floods of foreigners invading while you can do nothing.

Wicked men wanna get in your home cuz there you're in control and they want your gold.

DIVERSITY IS CRUELTY

Mexicans call black people names. They look down on em, the myth they get along is just fake.

There is no multicultural unity, they hate each other.

They push a false idea we all get along and it's NOT TRUE!

TRASH BIN: AFTER WE INVITED EM IN

We invited them into our home and they turned, giving us the finger. Make em go back/no linger.

Our differences don't make us stronger it's our similarities bringing us together to storm the weather.

Affirmative action is at a crossroads. Trump said we'll no more use race as a diversity code.

The dirty dems wanna bring millions more in and they can do any awful thing they'll be forgiven.

Evil is dissolving every minute. It's a snowball effect as Trump was in it. A bad memory, forget it.

Trump offers Pocahontas ONE MIL to prove Indian heritage as audacity destroys arrogance

Socialism always ends in poverty and violence but you think this time it won't/why take a chance?

What would you do if a million foreigners walked thru your land and pooped everywhere, man?

Not just "demographic change" but moving from happy light to depressed dark/not about skin color.

What would you do if a foreign mob trudged thru your front yard and killed your cats and dogs?

We gotta keep em out--they're not refugees but economic migrants, just want the money honey.

DIVERSITY IS CRUELTY

One damnable heresy is forgiveness without repentance, making em into recidivist criminals.

If you want open borders you hate blacks, cuz illegal immigrants are taking their jobs and tax.

Those who are part of this world are Prophets of Baal.

There's a plan in place and it's all gonna happen so prepare for panic and great civil unrest even.

The royal wedding not a celebration of England but multiculturalism and cultural Marxism.

Whites celebrating diversity are rejoicing at their declining numbers and influence, a monstrosity.

KAREN KELLOCK BOOKS:

AFFINITY OR MISERY
AGELESS CORNUCOPIA
AMERICA AWAKE!
AMERICA'S DAFT ERA
ARTS OF PALEO FASTING
AUTOPHAGY ON CHEATERS
BACKSTABBING NEUROTICS
BETRAYAL TRAUMA
BOOMERS AND BROKENNESS
BOOT ON NECK
CHAMPION GUIDES
COMMIE NUTHOUSE
COMMIES
COMMUNIST SPIRIT
CONTAGION OF MADNESS
CONTAGIOUS MADNESS
CULTURE CLASH BASHED
DAFT LEFT
DAILY FASTARIAN
DAM RATS
DIVERSITY IS CRUELTY
E-RACE WHITE
THE END OR A BEND?
FEMALE BULLIES AND FEMI-NAZIS
FEMALE CARNALITY
FEMALE DUMB DOWN
FEMINISM AND RUIN 1 & 2
FIX FOR MISFITS
FOOLS & TRAMPS
FREEDOM SPEAKING
FRENEMY ENABLER
FRENEMY LIAR
FRENEMY THIEF
FRENEMY TRAITOR
TRENEMY TYRANT
GENIUS IS HELD DOWN
GLOBALISLAM
GOD USES THE FLAWED
HAZE OF THE LATTER DAYS

THE HERD IN WORDS
HIX POLITIX
HOW THEY RUINED US
JUST SKIP DINNER
LE FEMME AND THE COMMUNIST SPIRIT
LIBERAL CHAOS & ROT
LIBERAL DOUBLETHINK
LIBERAL GALL 1 & 2
LIBERAL SHOVE-DOWNS
LOCK YOUR GATE
MANUAL FOR SUPERIOR MEN
MODERN ART FROM HELL
MOSTLY FAKE
NOTES TO CHAMPS 1 & 2
OVERCOME FRENEMIES
PC MAKES US CRAZY
PEOPLE ARE CRUEL
PEOPLE PROBLEMS 1 & 2
PERSECUTED GENIUIS
POLI-PSYCH MYSTERIES
PRETENTIOUS SLOBS
QUEEN BEE
RETURNING TO FIRST NATURE
THE SCHOOLS SCREWED EM UP
SEASON OF TREASON
SEPARATE MEANS HOLY
SOCIAL HYPNOTISM
SOLITUDE SOLUTION
SUPERCILIOUS
TOAD TO PRINCE
TRIALS CYCLES
TRUMP VS. GROUP
TRUST IN TRASH
THE TRUTH ABOUT PEOPLE
UNDERHEANDEDLY CLEVER
WALK TALL WITHIN WALLS
WE'RE NOT ALL ONE
WINNERS SKIP DINNER
WORK OR SMERK

AUTHOR BIO

Karen Kellock Ph.D.

Ph.D Political Psychology, UCI 1976
Post-Doctoral: UCI Medical School
Department of Psychiatry
Grants NIMH, NIAAA

Ph.D. dissertation "A Systems-Theoretic View of Pathologic Interaction" made an early mark as the "Wife of the Alcoholic Syndrome". Postdoctoral research at UCI Medical, Dept. of Psychiatry on the systems surrounding pathology on NIMH and NIAAA federal grants: *The Contagion of Madness: The Psychology of Neurotic Interaction and Pathological Systems*. Therapy tool Therapeutic Playwriting introduced the play *Mary and Murv: Gruesome Twosomes in the Alcoholic Marriage*. She taught Abnormal Psychology and Pathological Systems Theory at UC and CSU campuses and developed "the Debris Theory of Disease" in five books and website: (www.karenkellock.org): *Champion Guides, Daily Fastarian, Just Skip Dinner, Arts of Paleo Fasting, Ageless Cornucopia. Manual for Superior Men is a* pick-it-up-anywhere book that you can't put down (20,000 Kellockialisms) and ever on your desktop it should be found (or this Ebook for superior wordsearch of new jargon).